DISAVOWED

DISAVOWED

Refined in the Fire of Divorce

A . M . H O U S T O N

ISBN-13: **9780692858462**
ISBN-10: **0692858466**

ACKNOWLEDGMENTS

To my beautiful God: my Protector, Comforter, and Healer in the fire.

Geninne Zlatkis:
I am infinitely grateful for the generous contribution
of your time and talent to the cover art.

Barbara Houston-Silva
Ektor Silva
Steve King
Allegra Chatterjee-Gang
Nikki Kluj
Jasmine Dadarwala
Maria Cignarale
Von Marie Streubel
Juli Collins-Thompson
John Emerson
Jonathan Betlinski
Guillaume Bonnard

Thank you all for your love and support on this journey.

CONTENTS

FOREWORD

A. M. Houston and I first met in our twenties, when friendships were fluid and flirtatious by nature. Intriguingly, she refused stereotypes. Then, as now, she chose differently, lived differently. Loyal. Determined. Decidedly optimistic. Hungry for a place to rest without fear of being overrun or otherwise overlooked. Always clear in her devotion to God, to words, and to the power inherent in each.

My favorite moments as a psychiatrist happen when someone I've just met trusts me enough to invite me alongside them as they walk through the most human parts of their lives—the gritty, messy, vulnerable, raw, triumphant, and terrifying chapters that no one else gets to read. No one is a poet in those moments, yet the best sonnets capture less truth about our hearts. Each story amazes me and teaches me, too. Each journey leaves me heartbroken, happy, and humbled by the honesty and healing that happen. Far from scarring or scaring me, each glimpse of the world through the eyes of another nudges me to accept the next invitation.

Consider this book your invitation, then, to spend a few minutes—or months, maybe—walking alongside one of the strongest people I know. *Disavowed* details the author's gut-wrenching battle to move from abandonment to abundance. It is an unvarnished critique of things commonly held sacred by poets. You may sob. You will learn.

Jonathan Betlinski, MD
Clinical Associate Professor
Director, Division of Public Psychiatry
Oregon Health & Science University

Comfort…

"For thy Maker is thine husband;
For the Lord hath called thee as a woman
forsaken and grieved in spirit,
and a wife of youth,
when thou wast refused,"
saith thy God.

Isaiah 54: 5–6 (KJV)

BILL OF RIGHTS

You have the right to your feelings.
It needn't be pretty.
It needn't be approved by anyone else.
You have the right to feel every emotion that you're feeling.
You have the right to mourn and to do so without being judged.
No one has the right to tell you what your mourning should look like
or how long it should take.
This is your journey.
No one else can walk it for you.
Remember to be good to yourself.

It takes both sides to bring about the demise of the relationship.
Remember that we are imperfect people,
who endeavored to become one.
Sometimes, a spouse cannot live up to the task.
Sometimes, you cannot live up to the task.
Remember to forgive.
Forgive them, and forgive yourself.
Forgiveness is not a feeling.
It is a decision.
When forgiveness is the hardest to give,
that is when you most need to give it.
This is a test of love,
but if you really loved,
you can do this,

no matter how much it hurts.
Forgiveness holds the key to your healing.

It hurts like hell at the beginning.
You may want to die in the middle.
But you will not always feel that way.
Change your thoughts.
You can choose that option.
Think about the things that make you happy.
The end of a marriage is not the end of your life.
There will still be happy days ahead for you.
There will be beauty again.
There will be things that will make you laugh and dream.
There will be days that will make you glad once more to be alive.
You have everything to live for.
Be good to yourself.

BREAKDOWN

I work all day.
I put away the spreadsheets and walk into the kitchen.
I put thought into making your dinner:
braised short ribs on an ordinary Wednesday night,
cornish hens and coconut mashed yams.
You don't see the love that went into preparing your food.
You don't see the clean house,
the clothes washed, folded, and put away in their place.
You will not look at me.
You do not see me.
You do not hear me.

I cannot get you off the phone
with the woman you are talking to—
the one who knows her ascendancy is guaranteed,
because you have ceded her the place
that belongs to your wife.
She knows what you have done.
She knew it when you brought her to meet me.
She looked me up and down
and scornfully muttered, "Oh, so you do exist."
With five little words,
she declared war on your household.
And you gave her your colors to fly, Marine.

And the wife who followed you through states
and changes of duty stations,
who left her work, family, and friends
to be your support,
you do not rate important enough
to speak to first of possible deployments.
The one who would have to care for you
if you lost a limb,
or your mind,
is the one you dishonored with your secrets.

You broke my heart.
And then you tried to break me,
isolate and bury me in trench warfare.
I am not your prisoner of war, Marine.
I will not let you,
the woman who strategically left her underwear in my closet,
or your mother destroy me.
And you can tell your mother:
I am somebody's daughter,
and I too am beloved.

She wields her mouth as a weapon against me
to destroy our household.
She ever plays the martyr
as she plunges the knife into my back.
She would do well to remember that she too has a daughter.
And life has a way of working out its own justice.

Since she needs her son to love her
more than he loves his wife—
since you have forgotten you made a vow to me at the altar,
not to your mother—
she can keep you.
It is clear to me
no other woman can.

MASSACRE

That day, that night I uncovered the lie.
I was a wife, astonished and bitterly wounded
by the artfully constructed siege of my territory.
Done in the dark,
by combatants whose very name I bore.
I was a queen.
But as with all men who lack understanding of their woman,
he tried to strip my crown
and make me…ordinary.

He attempted to destroy me from the inside out.
He took aim at my womb.
"I don't want to have a child with you," he said.
Not with his wife.
Then he struck my foundation.
He told me I was nothing.
That no one cared for me.
That I need to be…other.
A version of myself that could be controlled
by his insecurities and weakness,
in order to please him.

If I were a different woman,
he may have very well succeeded.
I started to believe him.
I came to the courts of broken-down covenants
as a broken woman.
But in the process of being discarded,
that crucible
regenerated determination and self-respect in my blood.
It made the thought of allowing a man to destroy me anathema.
And I stood my ground,
for my life.

WRESTLING

The days go on and on.
No word from you.
Today, I grew angry.
You alone are deciding our fate.
Our fate.
You have determined I am not your equal in this marriage.
So I must sit and wait
and eat the bitter words you cast at me,
while you alone get to decide what is to become of us.

You are punishing me
when it was your own crime.
I did not go off with her in secret.
You tell me I am at fault.
I didn't see what I saw.
I didn't hear what I heard.
I am full of misunderstanding; she is a friend.
You would tell your distressed wife
you are not accepting an ultimatum
to end your relationship with this woman,
even to the detriment of your marriage.

You demand of me that I should keep no friends, no family,
no record of anything that came from you.
I did not ask the same of you.
I asked only for some of your time and a little understanding,
things too hard to give to your wife.
Your silence tears at my heart.
And my despair is turning into rage.

YOU ARE NOT MY RIVAL

You were an exit strategy.
He was too weak to set boundaries around his home.
He lacked the integrity to end his marriage with respect,
so he used you as the final trigger to destroy it.

The wrong was his;
still, it hurt to discover you.
I will not hold onto anger toward you.
In life, we all have made choices we later come to regret.
But sorrow is inevitable,
when your happiness is built
upon the pain of another woman.

Learn who a man is
before you trust him with your heart.
Love yourself better.
Give that gift to yourself.

FRAILTY

My cup is empty and needs to be replenished
with something other than my tears.
I want a life that sings and overflows with joy and hope—
a life that wants me in it.

My strength fails me at present.
I am so tired.
Will I lose this battle?
The only words my soul feels
pour out of my wounds like an unrelenting rain,
pounding out of my heart in blood.

I have no will to continue, but I have to find it.
I have to call it to me.
I have to get up.
There are still more loves out there to break my heart.
But if it is already broken and stays that way,
no one else can break it.

I am lonely, and I am hurting.
How could I have allowed my husband to wound me so deeply?
How careless of me
not to have better guarded my heart
from my heart.

This cannot be the way that my story ends.
I will not lie down and die.
I cannot give up on myself.
My life is still precious.
I am still valuable,
and I am worth fighting for.

TO MY CHILD, WHO IS NOT

You are not yet made.
You are just a hope I have had for a very long time.
My husband,
the man I shared my life with,
did not want to be a father.
I am sorry, my love, that it took me so long to find this out.
I wasted so much time.

I went to the doctor's office today.
In front of a stranger,
my tears burned a hole in my womb.
I asked him what I could do
to preserve my ability to bring you into this world.
He offered me science.
But I cannot imagine raising you without a father.
I do not want that for you.

I did not make good choices for you.
Waiting for the right timing,
I never gave you the chance to be.
Now, I am out of time.
A regret I will carry for the rest of my life.

Forgive me, my love.

BITTER ROOT

These hands, small and brown,
carry my history.
Scarred by hours, days, months, and years
when I lacked any covering,
so that sorrows and hardship
had their way with me.
I wonder—if I could, would I trade those times
for a gentler start?
But I hate weakness.
And I respect the warrior
He has been fashioning out of me
since I have known myself in this world.

Of late, though,
I am troubled.
Out of me seems to have gone
every sweetness, every softness.
I was tough
but always kind.
Now, I do not care to be.
Perhaps I have forgotten how to live
and only know how to survive.

I am afraid of bitter root
and bitter fruit.
I am afraid of yielding fertile ground
to a destructive vine.
I need to cling to heaven's hand,
think less about the womb that was never filled
or the years taken by deception,
when it might have been.

CAUTERIZE THE WOUND

So many conflicting emotions.
I feel angry.
I feel sad.
I feel afraid to let go,
afraid to cut the cord,
afraid of the finality of signing the paper and what it means.

He wants nothing of me.
Not to know me.
Not to love me.
He broke his promises to me.
He broke all of them, one by one,
sometimes in threes.

He promised me his love, his fidelity.
I ate it up like an orphan child.
Then, after I believed,
he orphaned me again.
I feel numb,
exhausted from pain.
I want the bleeding to stop.
For good.

BATTLE

I was present.
I did not run away.
I took the fall.
I stood up.
I wrestled for new ground.
Blows rained upon me with fury.
I wept.
I prayed.
I stood up.
I wrestled for new ground.

With torches and flaming swords, they gathered,
Mouths dripping with the breach.
I crawled through the trenches,
battered and broken.
I bled.
I wept.
I prayed.
I stood up.
I wrestled for new ground.

And so it wore on,
month after month.
Time congealed into a scab.
And then one day,
I noticed I was sturdier,
that the losses did not consume me,
did not take me down as often,
for as long.
Out of weariness came resilience.
Out of a broken heart came hope.
Out of battle came strength.
Out of fire came gold.

SIGNING OF THE PAPERS

An elementary prayer spoken,
then the flash of a sterling-silver Cartier pen.
A private ritual to observe the solemnity of loss.
A signature to end a marriage.

There were two at the altar,
yet only one mourns.
There was a gathering for the union
but not for the dissolution.
That is a singular path to be treaded alone,
in blood and in fire.

Our lives are marked by time and witness
and, sometimes, by tears.
For better or for worse.

DISAVOWED

He left.
Not in a respectful way.
Not in a mature way
that involved discussion,
face-to-face,
bare emotions on the table.
He took no consideration of the commitment made.
No thought of the intimacy of the covenant
created that beautiful evening in early December,
before God and our families.
It never dawned on him that he and I
were now a family.
Only his blood mattered.

He tore us asunder.
Betrayal does not heal seamlessly.
You will heal, but a scar will remain—
the way a broken thing will never go back to its unbroken state
after the breaking has taken place.
You may look at that scar as a disfigurement,
a sign of rejection,
of failure.
But that would not be the whole truth.
If you were rejected, it was because he never saw you.

One day, it will not matter
who was right or wrong,
innocent or guilty.
What will matter most is forgiveness.
You will have to find a way to give it to him,
or that thing will never let you go.
You deserve better than to remain broken.
At some point, you will realize that he is a broken man.
Perhaps if he knew what love was,
he could have loved you better.
But you knew by looking at the one who taught him that
he could not have known how.

Forgive him.
Forgive them all.
Get up.
Go on.
It is OK to imagine a new life for yourself.
And it is OK to trust
and let your heart stay tender
so that you might let love in.

SWIM

All of life and its struggles,
the fight summed up in one word:
swim.

We each face different demons,
different burdens.
None of us is exempt.
But we have to get up after falling.
We have to dust off the knees,
collect our hearts and our thoughts,
rein in every single particle of grit
in our soul, and carry on.
Swim.

Waking or dreaming,
through doubt or failure,
anger or pain—
swim.

It's the only thing we can do
to propel us forward,
to come out on the other side,
where, sometimes, just surviving
is the victory.

WHEN YOUR HEART IS WEARY

When it comes, the fear,
you tell it to go.
When it comes, the sorrow,
you tell it to go.
No matter where they cut you
or how deep the wound,
you owe a debt to yourself to survive.
One day, you will move past just surviving;
you will live again.

Courage is whispering your name.
She is the one urging you not to give up.
Listen to her.
She means you well.
The voices that rose up to silence yours
and destroy your spirit—
those, you abandon.
The pathology of rejection is simple.
An enemy meant to destroy you.
But will you let it?
No.

You will get up.
You will hold on.
You will fight for yourself.
You are valuable.
Your life is worth the life you gave.
More, even.
If you cannot silence their voices,
use them as a foothold to rise above
the defeat they wish for you.
You were never theirs,
and they will never be yours.

REMEMBER TO FORGET
(OUR ANNIVERSARY)

Today, I'll put on the red dress.
I'll wear gold at my throat
and on my wrists.
I'll put on the fishnets and high heels.
I'll curate my beauty, for myself.

But I prayed first.
I prayed for my heart
not to become hard.
I prayed for a real love to come
that is honest, mature, and kind.

I prayed to forget the white dress
I never wanted to wear.
I prayed to forget
the moment you placed the ring on my finger
and your vow.
The words were just words.

I prayed to forget
the effervescent bubble of joy that enveloped us
after we stole away from the chapel.
Just the two of us.
No words.

None needed.
We were lit from inside
with fragments of stars.
We burned in love
and in awe of each other.
But you burned out.

I grieve, but there is no body to bury.
Dreams are hard to bury,
harder to forget.
Covenants are broken every day,
this one no different from any other,
except that it was mine.

I'll die for you, you said.
But one who does not know true love
cannot offer it sacrificially,
despite the best of intentions.
I herald the night.
It can best hide my tears, and in it,
I can work on remembering to forget
all that we lost,
together.

CAKE

It appeared that you did not love me,
so I had to stop loving you.
If I could not manage that,
at the very least, I must leave you.
In truth, you left me long before I realized it.

So I gave you back your name,
and I reclaimed my mind.
I surely must have lost it to let you
take me on that joyless ride.

I only wanted a cake for my birthday
and an early morning call.
Not a catalog of why I was not
good enough to receive either
or the reasons why the motorcycle you bought yourself
on my birthday was more affordable than a cake,
in your selfish philosophy.

Now I make my own happiness,
as I did before you.
I no longer wonder
why I wasn't enough for you.

I am fortunate that love surrounds me now.
But my birthday sometimes reminds me of a day,
one of several you tendered,
when I felt least loved in the world among women.

I needed you to say that you were sorry for hurting me
and to mean it.
But I know that day will never come.
So I will make my peace
as best I can with this time.
You and the others that you let in
couldn't destroy me,
because I am too full of love to drown.
Love lifts me up.
It keeps me alive.

OUT OF FIRE, GOLD

The Lord returned my freedom back to me,
two years ago today.
At the time, I wept bitterly.
It looked like betrayal.
It looked like rejection.
It looked like a stunning loss.
Today, I can appreciate it for what it was:
pruning,
an opportunity for development,
the cultivation of mental and physical toughness,
the kind no one will ever destroy
because the Lord built it.

I am proud of this woman
who stares back at me in the mirror.
There are lines now on my face I didn't have before
and gray hair at my temples
and an unbreakable spirit
that will never, ever go down for the count.

I cherish this precious life that is mine.
I value my time and my gifts.
I am grateful to my Creator
for keeping my heart beating.
And I am learning to love myself
as no man will ever love me.
To life.

TURNING

We count the hours.
We divide the time
until the life imagined begins.
It begins with the courage to take the first step.

We know this for a truth:
if we do not try, we will never succeed.
In life, as in love,
rejection or its root, fear,
will keep us from our appointed destinies.

We must be fully persuaded
that the stirring in our heart,
which cries out for more,
is the driver of our liberation.
But we must be willing to do the work,
and the work is to believe.

DISCLOSURE

I didn't write these words to hurt you.
I wrote to get the hurt out of me
so that it didn't kill me.
I had to survive.

I didn't follow your story.
The birds of the air brought me news.
I never sought it.
I cried for ten months unceasing.
I cried until I was broken,
to the point where I was dry.
You hurt me.
Deeply.

I don't have pretty words for you.
My words reflect your behavior.
But I am sorry.
I know that somewhere you won't want to recognize,
my words will hurt you too.
For that I am truly sorry.
I do not want to intentionally cause you any pain.

I forgive you.
I do.
And that is the last "I do"
I will ever say to you.

A NOTE

These poems represent two years of pain and loss turned into survival and healing.

I never intended to share my story. But edit after edit, I saw that out of a time of great darkness, a song of strength and courage emerged. I want to encourage you that you have the ability to see your trial through. There is a seed of resilience buried deep within each one of us, but it requires the hardness of trial to develop and spring forth.

Get up, beloved. Hold your head up. Walk through the fire.

A promise...

And the desert shall rejoice, and blossom as the rose...

Isaiah 35:1 (KJV)

A. M. Houston entered New York University at the age of sixteen, and graduated as a Kappa Tau Alpha honoree with a degree in journalism. She has worked for the past two decades in the fashion industry.

www.ingramcontent.com/pod-product-compliance
Lightning Source LLC
Chambersburg PA
CBHW031542040426
42445CB00010B/659